Published by
MAE Dixon, LLC
311 Autumn Lake Dr
McDonough, GA 30253
(850) 554-4663

Other publications at http://
maedixon.com

All Scripture taken from The Message
(MSG); The NIV Bible; The KJV Bible/…
Used by permission of NavPress
Publishing Group

ISBN - 978-1-7353725-8-7
ISBN – 978-17353725-9-4

Crown Me Queen

for I am

Precious, Powerful

& Majestic

By Mae Dixon

My Personal Journal

Crown Me Queen

- for I am Precious, Powerful & Majestic

My Personal Journal

It's a blueprint to help young girls prepare for adulthood while experiencing their time as adolescents and into their teen years.

This journal offers real life and real time instruction in a

language that most girls can understand and apply to daily life.

Life for women can be very difficult, it's those tools that girls

learn in her early years that will prepare them for their future.

This journal is one of the many tools used
by the author as part of the Youth
Leadership Development Program offered
by A Will & Way, Inc. For more information
about her other resources visit http://
www.maedixon.com

This Journal

Belongs to

This is Your-Story

Each day or as you are inspired to, take a few moments to sit and write your thoughts.

This journal is only a prompt. You may use the topics provided or create your own, add additional paper as needed or request another journal.

You are your thoughts, go back occasionally to see what you've written and see the progress you've made along the way.

A Letter of Love

Greetings,

What is it that you admire most in this life? Is it your good looks, long pretty hair, curvy body? Or is it the fact that underneath all of that there's a heart that ache for others more than oneself; a mind that is focused on making a difference in the world by stocking up on wisdom and knowledge.

Life can be a double edged sword. On the one side everything is smooth and easy, there's not a care in the world. While, on the other hand there's much work and sacrifice to be had for the most basic accomplishments.

When one has a full view of what's behind them, the present and what's happening now there is no need to apply oneself; no fret, no care, no effort...
However, since we don't know what's before us and can only guess at the present at times; we should be diligent in preparing ourselves.

Everything comes with a price. Your birth cost someone something, if nothing more than the pain endured by your mother to get you here. For every decision you make, no matter your age, you must stop to consider the cost of that decision; at that moment and into the future. "If I do *this* (act) what will the consequences be?" Right now a "moment" seems like a long time but I promise you, the time will be far greater and the consequences more costly if you fail to use it wisely.

I call you my sister because *you are* my sister (in love), and because I love you. I want you to live a long, happy and prosperous life. Trouble will come but because you will have attained (Godly) wisdom and knowledge it won't overwhelm you.

TABLE OF CONTENTS

AFFIRMATIONS

I am the head and not the tail

I was bought with a price (by God)

I will honor my mother, father and elders so that I may enjoy a long life

I am a leader not a follower

I am a child of the king.

I can do all things through Christ who gives me strength.

I am more than a conqueror.

To love myself is the greatest
gift to the world.

I surround myself with people
who affirm me.

My circle consist of those who
lift me up.

I give more than I take.

The simplest prayer is, "Lord,
help me."

We all must believe in
something, let it be in a living
God who protects and provide
for our daily needs.

MEDITATION

When all else fails, seek peace within, doing so will give
You clarity and a calm that surpasses all understanding.

"Meditation is a technique such as mindfulness, the focusing on a particular object, thought, activity to train attention and awareness, to achieve a mentally clear and emotionally calm and stable state." (Wikipedia)

Centering Prayer is a surrendering method of meditation, that reaches back to the early days of Christianity.

To do this form of meditation: Find a quiet space where you are unlikely to be disturbed.
• Sit in a way that allows you to be relaxed in body and alert in mind. Use a chair, meditation cushion or prayer rug, according to your own physical needs and preferences.

• Gently close your eyes.

- • "Allow your heart to open toward that invisible but always present Origin (God)of all that exists "

- • • Whenever you become aware of a thought, no matter what its nature, let it go.

• Use a "sacred word".

This is a word or short phrase that helps you to let go of thoughts. It is a reminder of your intention to remain open to the silence. Generally sacred words fall into one of 2 categories: "God" words/ phrases such as "Abba", "Jesus, "Mary", "Reality", "Come Lord" or "state" words/ phrases such as "love", "peace", "be still". Sacred words are not used as mantras, as in constantly repeating them, but as a reminder of your intention to remain open.

• Continue this practice for 20 minutes. At the end of the time get up and go about your business, leaving the practice behind, in the same way you let go of your thoughts.

• People who are just beginning, and are particularly restless in mind and body, may find it easier to start off with shorter prayer periods, perhaps only 5 minutes per sit to start. Then after a few days extend the time to 10 minutes and so on until you are able to sit for 20 minutes. Give the practice at least 2 weeks before you decide if it is right for you.

• Two 20-30 minute sits per day are considered ideal. It is strongly recommended that no one meditates for more the 60 minutes a day unless you are attending a structured retreat with an expert.   Source: CONTEMPLATIVE.ORG

GIFT

You have a gift called "Youth" right now. Use it wisely, be smart, be generous with your love to your fellow man but, love and respect yourself *first* . Spend wisely. Let your adornment be a healthy body and the beauty will shine through. Things do not bring happiness, peace nor joy, nor does it make the person, but people who love you do.

Achieve great things, you were born for a purpose, you have a gift(s) that is unique to you. Find out what it is and use it/them to the fullest potential. Don't allow others to bring you down to their level. If they're not willing to step up then leave them where they are.

You are destined for greatness and
don't allow anyone to distract you.
Don't confuse greatness with
money or fame, greatness comes
from within and is everlasting.
Money comes from the world and
is most often temporal. There's
many a bum who is filled with
greatness but lost their way
because they allowed money and
fame to define and corrupt them.

Wait for love - don't be in a hurry
to find a girlfriend, Take the time
to know who you are and then to
know who she is. The girlfriend/
mate for you has already been
determined, there is no need to
experiment with every girl that
makes herself available. You will
find her and she will bring with
her the ingredients for a real love
relationship. The acceptance of

anything less is a prescription for disaster.

No one is perfect - mistakes will happen, recognize that it's a mistake, do what, if anything is needed to be done to correct it and move on.

When in doubt, seek help. Counsel is available in many forms - parental, peer, pastor, school officials, psychological and most important godly. Keep a bible handy, download the app; in it you will find instruction, wisdom, inspiration and peace for every situation.

Peace,
Ms Mae

Life is not about regrets, but preparations.

A Life well lived is GOLDEN.

I'm writing my own story

The rest of this Journal is designed to encourage, inspire and motivate to

document your personal journey as you navigate this thing called life each day.

In doing so you will find that life is less stressful when you take the time to write

down your thoughts.

Sometimes you may find it helpful to just write mindlessly (without thinking),
walk away and then return later to see what was written and determine if you still feel that way.

Your journal is a judgement-free zone.

If you feel troubled by some of the things you think or write don't be afraid to talk

about it with someone you trust such as

a parent, aunt, mentor, best friend or a doctor.

Strangers stab you in the back,
boyfriends stab you in the heart,

but true friends poke each other
with straws.

We are born into this world not
to be perfect,

but to be ourselves.

____

____

____

____

____

____

____

____

____

____

____

____

____

____

My thoughts today

I'm beautiful. I'm strong. I'm unique.

I won't let anyone tell me otherwise.

\-------------------------------------

\-------------------------------------

\-------------------------------------

\-------------------------------------

\-------------------------------------

\-------------------------------------

\-------------------------------------

\-------------------------------------

\-------------------------------------

\-------------------------------------

\-------------------------------------

\-------------------------------------

\-------------------------------------

\-------------------------------------

\-------------------------------------

I cannot allow others to get into
my head and dictate my thoughts

Everyone is born with the same
amount of potential, it's

up to you to decide what to do
with it.

Draw a picture of your thoughts

Maybe you have to let go of who you were to become who you're

meant to be.

Write the lyrics to your favorite song

It hurts when your friend gets a
boyfriend and then

they slowly forget about
everyone else.

What would your future look
like if you could choose it today

A boys' laugh is much more
cheerful than a girls'.

But a girls' tears are much more
meaningful than a boys'.

You get what you give

If people are trying to bring you
down,

it means you're above them.

Our friends are a shelter where
we feel free to be ourselves

Sometimes I just want to be
alone,

but people start talking to me.

I Am Valuable

I'm single not because I don't
pray for love.

I'm single because I don't play
with love.

— — — — — — — — — — — — — — —

— — — — — — — — — — — — — — —

— — — — — — — — — — — — — — —

— — — — — — — — — — — — — — —

— — — — — — — — — — — — — — —

— — — — — — — — — — — — — — —

— — — — — — — — — — — — — — —

— — — — — — — — — — — — — — —

— — — — — — — — — — — — — — —

— — — — — — — — — — — — — — —

— — — — — — — — — — — — — — —

— — — — — — — — — — — — — — —

— — — — — — — — — — — — — — —

— — — — — — — — — — — — — — —

— — — — — — — — — — — — — — —

I am strong and courageous

Be careful of who you trust, the devil was once an angel.

Determination is doing what
needs to be done even when you
don't feel like doing it.

Deep down we all need that one person. No matter how

much we deny it. It's a fact that remains unchanged.

Maturity is not when we start speaking big things. It is when we start understanding small things.

There are no hopeless situations

Only people who think
hopelessly.

_ _ _ _ _ _ _ _ _ _ _ _ _ _

_ _ _ _ _ _ _ _ _ _ _ _ _

_ _ _ _ _ _ _ _ _ _ _ _ _ _

_ _ _ _ _ _ _ _ _ _ _ _ _ _

_ _ _ _ _ _ _ _ _ _ _ _ _ _

_ _ _ _ _ _ _ _ _ _ _ _ _ _

_ _ _ _ _ _ _ _ _ _ _ _ _ _

_ _ _ _ _ _ _ _ _ _ _ _ _ _

_ _ _ _ _ _ _ _ _ _ _ _ _ _

_ _ _ _ _ _ _ _ _ _ _ _ _ _

_ _ _ _ _ _ _ _ _ _ _ _ _ _

_ _ _ _ _ _ _ _ _ _ _ _ _

_ _ _ _ _ _ _ _ _ _ _ _ _

_ _ _ _ _ _ _ _ _ _ _ _ _

_ _ _ _ _ _ _ _ _ _ _ _ _

_ _ _ _ _ _ _ _ _ _ _ _ _

I'm a Girl Boss

I hate it when I'm bored and
there isn't anything on TV,

but when I'm busy, everything
comes on.

You hurt me... so why do I still love you?

Me -vs- Me - I am my only competition

Not wanting to talk to anyone,
but at the same time

not wanting to be alone....

Things always seem impossible
until they get done.

Give thanks for what you are
now, and keep fighting

for what you want to be
tomorrow.

It isn't where you come from, it's
where you're going that counts.

Things will happen in your life
that you can't stop.

There's a purpose for the good
and for the bad.

To believe in yourself is
POWER!

Don't judge me for who my
friends are,

we are different people.

Today only happens once, how will you make it Amazing?

Goodbyes make you think. They
make you realize what

you've lost, what you have and
what you took for granted.

What can I do differently to change my current circumstances?

If a boy and girl are talking,
smiling and laughing together,

doesn't mean they are together!
They can be just good friends.

A best friend is someone you
grow up with....

A true friend is someone who
helps you grow up.

A messy room is a sign that you
have less control than you think.

I miss school during the summer, and I miss summer during school.

My best friend and I can speak to each other

through facial expressions.

I am my own unique beautiful self.

Life is nothing but challenges;
the more you succeed,

the more you learn.

There's only one panacea for
ALL our worries....

GOD.

I had a crush on a guy, and he was already taken.

I guess it was never meant to be.

Life throws sticks and stones at
you,

but they help you become who
you are today.

I am capable of great things,
some of them are........

A good life should always be
made,

not to be waited for.

I cannot allow others to bring me
down. I am enough.

Who am I?

My smile is my passport, my personality is who I am.

My Aspirations Are

Things I need to do to achieve my Aspirations are

We must keep encouraging one
another each day, it makes life
beautiful.

In life being fair or unfair
depends on how we think, we are

equally the same, we breathe in
the same air, we look upon

the same sky and we stand on the
same ground. What makes

us different is our perception in
life. How we're going

to cope with the difficulties of
life.

Never allow anyone to tell you that you don't matter.

NOTES

NOTES

NOTES

NOTES

NOTES

NOTES

NOTES

NOTES

NOTES

OOPS!

Did you run out?

No worries, order additional Journals

for yourself, your family and friends

at: <u>maedixon62@gmail.com</u>

include the following information:

Name, phone #, title of book/journal

and quantity desired.

About the author

Mae Dixon is the Amazon best-selling author of "The Secret Code of Girls – The Ins & Outs of Being a Female," " The Secret Code of Girls - Empowering Girls to Become Confident Women and "Restored by Grace - A Journey Like No Other". Dixon has also authored teen journals, poems, blogs and newsletters. Dixon has experienced a rewarding real estate career for over 40 years where she received numerous awards, public exposure (newspaper, magazines, podcasts & tv) for her expertise and peer leadership including Realtor of the Year and Top Gun in Real Estate. She is a certified spiritual healing coach and has written and facilitated numerous empowerment programs for women and youth. Dixon is a community advocate for survivors of domestic violence and social justice. She has founded and served on numerous boards and committees and received awards and recognition for her leadership. Dixon is the proud mother of two sons who blessed her with many grand and great-grandchildren.

Prior Work

Dixon has presided over and served on the Pensacola and Florida Real Estate Association Boards, The Community Drug and Alcohol Commission, Pensacola-

Escambia Citizens Law Enforcement Liaison Group, City of Clearwater Citizen's Academy, Pensacola Police Academy, Escambia County Sheriff's Academy, The Pensacola-Escambia Human Relations Commission, Escambia Board of Adjustments, Florida Supreme Court County Mediator,

Affiliations

National Assn of Female Executives, National Assn of Women Council of Realtors, Recipient of Congressional Award and Points of Light Award

Opportunities are available to teach leadership development based upon this journal. For training or speaking engagements email maedixon62@gmail.com or maedixon.com